SUSHI

for

BEGINNERS

A Complete beginner's Guide illustrated Step by Step! Discover
Features, Basics and How to Make Sushi at Home
by delicious Easy Recipes

OSAMI NISHIMURA

TABLE OF CONTENTS

INTRODUCTION

CONCLUSION

<u>INTRODUCTION</u>

Many people think that the word sushi means "raw fish," but this simply isn't so. A sushi dish may contain either raw or cooked fish. The word "sushi" actually does not refer to fish at all, but rather to the vinegared rice used in the dish. In Japanese the word for vinegar is "su" while the word for rice is "meshi."

So to say "vinegared rice" the two words are combined together as "sushi." When made correctly, the sweet vinegar used in the rice, should just contribute a very light flavor to the rice. It should not be bitter, tart, or "vinegary."

Sushi is as much an art form as it is a healthy and delicious food, and there are many ways of preparing it. It takes a lot of time, patience, and practice to perfect ones sushi making skills.

For the average person who is just getting interested in sushi, a sushi menu can be quite intimidating.

Maki-zushi, nigiri-zushi, and sashimi are just a few of the words you'll likely discover on a sushi menu.

DIFFERENT TYPES OF SUSHI

If you are new to sushi and don't know what the different types of sushi are yet, then hang on to your hat...

You're about to find out!

But first let's clear up a couple of little terms that sometimes can cause confusion for those trying to learn the distinction between the different types of sushi.

First, let's define exactly...

What is Sushi?

Sushi quite simply is "Anything that is made with vinegared sushi rice". Well, that's pretty easy to understand, huh?

So, what is Sashimi then?

People sometimes think that Sashimi is Sushi but it is not. And that is because it is not made or served with "vinegared sushi rice". Sashimi is just the meat all by itself.

Well, it may have some side items like shredded daikon (japanese radish) and ponzu sauce served with it, but normally that's pretty much it.

Definitely no sushi rice. So now that we know what sushi is and what it is not, we are ready to dig into the different types.

Maki-zushi or sushi roll

One of the most familiar forms of sushi found in restaurants is the maki-zushi or sushi roll. Here we find fish or seafood and/or vegetables rolled into vinegared rice and wrapped with a tender seaweed sheet called nori. The roll is then cut into slices.

When the nori is on the inside of the roll (an inside-out roll) it is referred to as uramaki. Some sushi restaurants also offer futomaki which is a much thicker roll than the standard maki-zushi.

Perhaps the most well-known of the maki-zushi rolls is the California roll. The California roll is usually made as a uramaki (inside-out) roll and often contains cucumber, imitation crab meat, and avocado.

It is then rolled in toasted sesame seeds, tobiko, or masago.

Tobiko is simply flying fish roe (eggs) and has a mild smoky/salty taste and is orange in color.

Masago is Capelin roe and has a similar taste and color.

<u>Nigiri-zushi or Nigiri</u> is made quite differently.

It generally consists of an oblong or rectangular mound of rice, topped with a piece of seafood such as salmon, tuna, eel, or octopus.

Nigiri is often made with raw fish. Many times the chef will add a small amount of wasabi between the rice and the seafood, and in some cases will wrap it together with a thin strip of nori.

Wasabi is known as Japanese horseradish.

It has an extremely strong flavor, and is usually light green in color. It only takes a tiny drop of wasabi to flavor sushi. Most sushi connoisseurs prefer not to use wasabi as its strong flavor can keep one from being able to taste the natural flavors of the sushi.

Sashimi is sliced raw fish. It is neither wrapped in a roll nor served on a bed of rice. It is sometimes served with shiso (a large green leaf) and daikon (shredded Japanese radish).

It's important to note that the sushi served in the Americas and Europe is very different than what is served in Japan and has been adapted over decades to appeal to the Western palate. So next time you're invited to "go out for sushi" give it a try. You just might like it.

The different types of sushi (in no particular order) are:

Makizushi

Nigirizushi

Inarizushi

Chirashizushi

Oshizushi.

Makizushi

Makizushi is the type of sushi that is rolled. Typically in nori, but can also be rolled in other things like a thin omelette, soy paper, cucumber and shiso (perilla) leaves.

Further defined, makizushi comes in 5 different kinds of rolls:

> Hosomaki ("thin roll"). Has rice on the inside and nori on the outside. Typically it contains 1 ingredient and is about 1 inch in diameter.

> Chumaki ("medium roll"). Has rice on the inside and nori on the outside. Usually 2 to 3 ingredients and about 1 ½ inches in diameter.

> Futomaki ("thick roll"). Has rice on the inside and nori on the outside. Comes in at 2 to 2 ½ inches in diameter with 4 or more ingredients.

➢ Uramaki ("inside-out roll"). Has rice on the outside and nori on the inside. The most popular example of this roll is the California Roll.

➢ Temaki ("hand-roll"). Which is a cone-shaped roll with nori on the outside and rice on the inside.

Nigirizushi

This form of sushi is the one with a slice of meat laying on a little oval pad of sushi rice.

Inarizushi

Inarizushi is a personal favorite of mine.

And it's too bad that many Americans, even those who consider themselves pretty well versed in sushi, have never had it.

This type of sushi is made by stuffing sushi rice into a seasoned, double-fried tofu pouch (called abura-age).

It has a slightly salty-sweet flavor that is hard to describe but is delicious.

<u>Chirashizushi</u>

Chirashizushi ("scattered sushi") is a type of sushi that is served in a bowl. It normally consists of sushi rice that is covered with various toppings, commonly totaling 9. It is popular in Japanese homes because it is simple to make and is ideal for using up leftovers.

Oshizushi

This type of sushi is made by layering sushi rice, toppings and condiments in a specially made box called an "Oshibako" and pressing the ingredients together to form a firm rectangular box of sushi. This rectangular box of sushi is then normally sliced into bite sized pieces before serving.

When it comes to sushi, a lot of people have a hard time taking that first leap and trying their first bite of raw fish. If you did not know, sushi is incredibly healthy when eaten in moderation; the oils from the fish have numerous benefits for your health and sushi in general is low in fat.

Here is some information about some of the most common rolls of sushi.

The California roll is as basic as it gets. This is without a doubt the beginners roll. After you have eaten sushi for a while, you will most likely move past this roll, unless it is being offered as an Hors D'oeuvres at a wedding or other type of party.

A salmon avocado roll is a great roll to get for several reasons. First and foremost, it is delicious. Second, both salmon and avocado have nutrients and oils that are very good for your skin. Finally, this roll is usually one of the cheaper options on a sushi menu.

While a yellowtail roll by itself may be a little bit bland, adding scallions to this roll will create a great texture. The yellowtail is silky and smooth while the scallion provides a nice amount of crunch.

One of the best ways to get an assortment like this is to get a rainbow roll, which usually has a variety of salmon, tuna, yellowtail and whitefish on top of crab, cucumber and avocado.

After you have graduated from the California roll, or if that just is not your thing, try a spicy tuna roll. Usually prepared with spicy mayonnaise, this roll is hard not to enjoy.

These are just some of the wonderful rolls to try in the world of sushi. Next time are trying to decide what to eat, branch out and try some sushi.

SUSHI NUTRITION:

IS SUSHI REALLY THAT HEALTHY FOR YOU?

The nutritional benefits of sushi is a subject that has long been debated and one that is often on the minds of sushi lovers.

It is also something pondered by those considering sushi as an alternative food source to incorporate into their diet for better health or maybe to offset the adverse effects of eating a normal western diet which is often high in unhealthy fats (trans and saturated), red meat, processed foods and calories.

But is sushi a better choice? Is it really healthy for you?

Perhaps the best way to make that determination is to take the most common ingredients used in making sushi and dissect them one by one.

Tear them apart and try to discover whether they actually are or are not healthy for you.

Let's begin with the most obvious dominant ingredient in this arena; and the one that is the very definition of sushi... Sushi Rice.

<u>Sushi Rice</u>

Rice is a good source of protein (1 cup provides 25% of RDA) and carbohydrates and digests slowly, releasing its energy gradually.

It is also gluten free (making it an excellent choice for those with wheat allergies), is very low in saturated fat, has no cholesterol or sodium, and is high in thiamin (vitamin B1).

Thiamine is a co-enzyme that helps the body convert carbohydrates into energy (glucose) causing it to be burned rather than stored.

This may partially explain why people in japan, where rice is eaten at almost every meal, have an obesity rate of just 3.2% which is about 10 times LESS than it is here in the United States.

Rice Vinegar

Rice Vinegar has long been accepted as having many medicinal health benefits in Japan for over 2,000 years. And all vinegars in general have been used in almost every country in the world for things ranging from flavoring and preserving rice, to a skin conditioner to its use in preventing cancer because of its anti-cancer properties.

Rice vinegar contains 20 different kinds of amino acids of which 9 are essential because they cannot be created from other compounds in the human body.

Some of Rice Vinegars purported health benefits include:

- Boosts the immune system

- Lowers cholesterol

- Increases the body's ability to absorb nutrients

- Lowers blood glucose levels

- Kills bacteria on contact such as salmonella and streptococcus

- Preserves food

- Reduces blood pressure

- Is gluten free

- Helps clear up urinary tract infections

- Reduces high blood sugar

- Aids in the relief of pain and symptoms from sunburn, jellyfish stings, insect bites, and headaches

- Helps to neutralize free radicals which damage cells that cause aging and degeneration

- Reduces cholesterol formation by neutralizing some of the harmful oxidized LDL cholesterol

With vinegar the list seems to go on and on and there seems to be no end to its posit

ive benefits on health.

Nori

Nori is very rich in vitamins and minerals. Especially iodine --- but also contains A, B1, B2, B6, niacin, and C. And compared to land plants, marine algae has as much as 10-20 times as much of these essential vitamins.

Nori is also known to help curb the formation of cholesterol deposits in the blood vessels and is high in protein (up to 50% of its dry weight).

It is also a good source of glutamic acid, an amino acid and a neuro transmitter, which is important for learning and memory.

Ginger

It has long been believed that ginger provides many beneficial medicinal advantages from aiding digestion, to preventing skin cancer, to eliminating nausea.

As a matter of fact, the Chinese prescribed ginger as a remedy for digestive issues over 3,000 years ago. And for centuries, the Ayurvedic tradition in Tibet and India used ginger to treat inflammatory joint diseases including arthritis and rheumatism.

Ginger has been used to treat ailments for thousands of years by cultures all over the world. It is one of the few foods that has withstood the test of time and one that is still being used today to treat the same ailments it was used to treat centuries and sometimes millennia ago.

The difference between then and now, is that now science and medicine are starting to support what some cultures have already known for hundreds or even thousands of years --- That ginger is indeed, as close to a cure all super root that we may ever discover.

Wasabi

Wasabi is known to have antibacterial properties and is also rich in Vitamin C, B6, protein, fibre and the minerals calcium, potassium, manganese and magnesium.

It also stimulates the production of saliva and aids in digestion. Wasabi also contains compounds called glucosinolates which is converted by enzymes into ITC's (isothiocyanates) if water is present when it is torn apart by chewing or being ground up.

There is current research that is starting to show that wasabi may be useful in controlling seasonal allergies and asthma and also may inhibit platelet aggregation (blood clotting) which could have applications in the treatment of heart attacks due to the ITC's.

There is also a growing base of evidence that ITC's may work against cancer cells.

Sushi Grade Fish

Most everyone has already heard about the benefits of eating fish versus other kinds of meat, especially red meat.

Just a small portion of fish supplies up to one half of the protein we require daily. It is also low in calories.

White fish such as sea bass and red snapper have less than 100 calories per 3 1/2 ounces. Mackerel, eel and tuna have less than 200 calories.

Oily fish such as Tuna, Salmon, lake trout, herring, and sardines are rich in Omega-3 fatty acids which can be effective in preventing heart disease, stroke and arthritis.

Eating just 2 servings of fish a week (about the size of a deck of playing cards per serving) could reduce your risk of dying of a heart attack. Especially if that fish is one that is high in Omega-3's.

In Japan, fish is eaten practically every day. No wonder heart disease and stroke are almost non-existent in Japan compared to the U.S. In Japan, heart disease deaths are around 30 in 100,000. By contrast, in the U.S. it is 106 per 100,000. Over 3 times higher.

Without a doubt, fish has to be one of the strongest ingredients contributing to the health benefits of eating sushi.

Vegetables

All kinds of vegetables are used in making sushi.

Vegetables are high in vitamins, minerals and fiber. In populations where a good quantity of fruits and vegetables are consumed, there are lower incidents of cancer. Plants also contain phytochemicals which help protect the body from disease.

And one of the best things about the vegetables used in sushi is that most of the time they are used in their natural raw state. Cucumbers, avocado, and carrots are usually sliced up and used raw. If they are cooked at all, normally they are only blanched. Spinach if used, is normally blanched.

All of this means that the vegetables used in sushi retain as many of the vitamins and minerals as possible because they are not cooked to death before being used.

Green Tea

For thousands of years and across almost every country in the known world, Green Tea has long been praised for its purported ability to improve health. From eradicating simple bacterial and viral infections to controlling or curing degenerative conditions such as stroke, cancer, cardiovascular disease, and osteoporosis the claims are many and some hard to believe. As a matter of fact, the evidence is so overwhelming that the chemo-prevention branch of the National Cancer Institute developed a plan for creating tea compounds to be used as cancer chemo-preventive agents in human trials.

KNOW THE ETIQUETTE OF EATING SUSHI BEFORE TRYING IT

Sushi is a very famous Japanese food that grew popularity in the United States just like it grew popular all over the world.

It has taken on some western flavors and techniques and this evolved sushi has traveled back to Japan to become trendy American Sushi.

There are some differences between the traditional sushi and the evolved American sushi. The first being that most of Japanese sushi had some sort of fish included, either raw or treated with pickles. American sushi has taken on a decidedly western technique when it comes to creation, adding area-specific ingredients and changing the shape, size and presentation format laid out by Japanese inventors.

It was very different from the sushi being served in Japan and America. As the food was then made through fermenting rice and fish, only the fish was eaten and the rice was not eaten, due to the sour taste. These days, this type of food is only served near Lake Biwa.

Japanese people invented modern sushi as finger food, so they could eat it without the use of chopsticks.

People would bring it at theater and at festivals to eat it with hands, thus the era of modern sushi came into existence.

As Japanese evolved sushi as food not to be eaten with chopsticks, many Japanese still like to eat it using chopsticks. Though Temaki is an exception. A Temaki is a nori roll shaped like an ice cream cone, and filled with variations.

Many other types include sukeroku, sashimi, nigiri, inari, oshi and maki. Americans also love these types of sushi and are familiar with them as these are served by many restaurants in America. In particular Sukeroku is very famously available in America because of vegetarian nature. Another name for this is ume sushi and it is considered as a low quality with ingredients available from common grocery stores.

Sukeroku is also a common type of sushi found in American grocery stores. It is a cheap food as it is vegetarian and has been Americanized.

Japanese and American sushi are also different as they are very different in quality. Sukeroku being a cheap sushi is widely available in America.

There are many bars in America that cater specifically to the American sushi craze, complete with loud rock and roll music.

This sort of sushi reflects what traditional Japanese diners would consider very outlandish ingredient combinations, and bars add to the atmosphere with American furnishings and color schemes.

10 ESSENTIAL THINGS TO KNOW BEFORE VISITING A SUSHI RESTAURANT

Are you a sushi beginner? Never been out for an evening of Japanese seafood dining? Then get yourself ready with the following essential information about how to get the most out of your sushi dining experience.

10 things to know about dining out for sushi

1. This is NOT Chinese food. Far too many people walk into a fine neighborhood sushi establishment and immediately request the Chow Mein special with a chicken egg roll. That's Chinese food, people. Sushi is a fresh, raw and healthy delicacy from Japan.

2. Watch out for the sake. Sake looks harmless enough; it is served from decorative bottles in tiny cups and glasses. But watch out for the alcohol kick from this strong spirit. To experience a sushi restaurant in full, enjoy a glass - but in keep it all in moderation.

3. Start with cooked menu items. It is a common misconception that all sushi is raw. Beginners may want to give cooked items such as California rolls or unagi (eel) a try before moving on to raw dishes.

4. Stick with what you know. Many of the types of fish you have enjoyed for years are available at a sushi bar - simply in raw form. If you like salmon or grouper - stick with their raw equivalent when ordering sushi for the first time.

5. Be prepared for the omakase. Omakase is loosely translated as "chef's choice" and ordering it puts you in the hands of the experienced sushi chef. Bear in mind, that while this option may indeed produce some delightful dishes, they may be a little too advanced for the novice palette.

6. Go veggie if you like. Did you know that you can eat a completely satisfying sushi dinner without eating any fish? It's easy if you stick to the vegetable rolls (such as the cucumber roll) and substitute veggies for seafood in other dishes.

7. It's good to ask questions. At some snootier fine dining establishments (French restaurants, we're looking in your direction) asking questions is frowned upon. However, at sushi bars, questions are encouraged. The best sushi chefs love to talk about their craft and share insight into the different dishes they will be serving.

8. Sushi is a healthy meal. Sushi is low in fat, filled with important nutrients and packed with vital protein. If you eat out once a week, it is much better for your body than a burger joint or chain restaurant.

9. Start the kids out young. The best way to raise a child with a sophisticated palette is to introduce them to different dishes at a young age. Taking them to a fun sushi restaurant is a great way to start them out on a life-long love of great seafood and Japanese cuisine.

10. You can enjoy sushi AND keep kosher. More and more, sushi restaurants are offering full kosher options as part of their menu. That means individuals who wish to maintain a strict adherence to their kosher diet can enjoy all the fun and good taste of a real sushi bar.

FINDING THE BEST PLACES TO BUY SUSHI

Sushi is an increasingly popular food item these days and many may wonder where the best place is to buy sushi. As more and more stores and restaurants are offering sushi to the raw fish buying public, purchasing the best type of sushi product is on the minds of sushi lovers everywhere. The following will list some of the more popular places to buy this delicacy and detail how to know which sushi is the best to purchase.

Restaurants Which Specialize in Sushi

As one may imagine, restaurants where the specialty is sushi is one of the best places to buy this type of food.

Not only will these restaurants have the best selection with regard to sushi entrees but they will also often have the freshest selection due to the popularity thereof.

A restaurant which goes through its food supplies quickly will often need to keep up a constant delivery of fresh ingredients in order to meet the demands of the sushi-eating patrons.

Restaurants Which Always Offer Sushi

Even restaurants which may not specialize in sushi but offer it on a constant basis might be a good choice as well.

Again, this type of restaurant which always offers sushi will have a fresh supply on hand constantly as it is a staple on the menu.

A restaurant which may have an occasional sushi special yet not have it as a permanent menu item might not be the best bet for those looking to buy sushi.

Grocery Stores with a Sushi Counter

More and more grocery stores are starting to offer sushi due to the increasing popularity of this item.

Not only are the grocery stores selling this product but they have a sushi counter installed around the deli area.

A grocery store with this type of section is another great place to visit for your sushi needs as it will often be freshly prepared by one who knows the art of sushi preparation.

Tips to Keep in Mind When Selecting Sushi Items

Now that one knows buying their sushi from a specialty restaurant, a restaurant which constantly offers sushi or a grocery store with sushi counter will often yield the best entrees, there are a few tips to keep in mind when buying this delectable food item.

First, know what you are eating. It is a good idea to inquire about the sushi contents prior to buying it so that you are getting exactly what you want and nothing which you do not wish to have.

Another tip to keep in mind is to inquire about its freshness. Find out when it was prepared, if purchasing from a grocery sushi counter, and only choose one which is extremely fresh. This will help you to find the freshest sushi out there and not take the chance of getting sick from fish which is not fresh.

Lastly, when buying various sushi items, try to expand your repertoire in the sushi department from time to time. Try various sushi plates in order to increase your varieties of sushi which you eat.

When you buy sushi, keep in mind that you don't know if you like it until you try it.

Many people are turned off by the thought of sushi, but probably because they were served less than perfect specimens of sushi. For anybody who's had both great and sub-par sushi, there is a constant struggle to differentiate the good restaurants from the bad. Some folks give up, determining that there's just no good sushi in their area, but this is almost never true.

If you understand the criteria, you can even find great sushi.

The first characteristic of a great sushi restaurant is that it specializes in sushi. Some restaurants advertise and focus on sushi, and other restaurants simply include sushi on their menu.

When sushi is not the focus, and just one of the hundreds of dishes the restaurant prepares, the quality of the sushi often suffers. A good example of this is buffets. If you've been to an Asian buffet that offers hundreds of food items, the small sushi section usually leaves much to be desired.

A great sushi restaurant, especially in a larger city, will usually be popular. A restaurant that gets very little foot traffic despite being in a busy area is usually avoided by the general public for a reason.

On the other hand, a great sushi restaurant will always be bustling, and will usually have a wait. If you'd rather not drive from restaurant to restaurant checking which have lines, you can also ask people who frequent or live in the area.

Another key to a good sushi restaurant, and restaurants in general, is how well it is maintained. Nobody wants to enjoy their food in a dirty broken-down dining area.

Not only is this off-putting to the eye, but it also reflects on the quality of the food. Fish is a delicate food to work with, and preparing in a dirty area can quickly lead to trouble.

SUSHI PRESENTATION

Japanese sushi has its own way of presenting in front of the purchasers. As you can see many of the food around the world, give much value to the way it is represented. So if you are a regular maker of sushi at home, it will be a good thought on put in some money on sushi plates so that you can also present it in a lovely way.

Most of the sushi chef equally consider the preparation and represent of sushi foods. So they definitely find time to select suitable utensil to present their food. To keep up the custom of sushi represent, you should also take care while selecting sushi plate set.

Along with sushi plates, you should also buy some more accessories which will then support the sushi plate set. matching chopsticks holders should be selected for the chop sticks, which is used to eat the sushi.

It will be attractive and more fitting if the chopsticks can be kept on the chopstick holders, rather than keeping them on the plate.

For keeping your soy sauce and wasabi, some appealing thin bowl should also be purchased. You can eat sushi after dipping the sushi in these side dishes which will give a appealing good flavor.

It is important that you take care of some points while eating the sushi. An additional use of soy sauce or wasabi will spoil the original flavor of sushi. Pouring these items more in to your sushi food is considered as insulting the sushi chef.

Hence you should take very small amount of soy sauce in to your plate and do not wasting it. Too much use of soy sauce and wasabi or wastage of these items is considered as rude behavior in sushi custom.

Along with the sushi plate, you should also buy a good quality tea set. It is traditional to serve green tea with sushi. Hence the use of an %attractive % and similar tea set will give a enjoyable look to the entire represent. At some places in Japan, a rice wine called sake is served instead of green tea.

Whatever be the drink along with the sushi, the selection of proper cups have an impact on the overall represent of the sushi. That is an important aspect in sushi food represent. If you do not have the time to sit and have the sushi food, rather than using the chop sticks, you can use your hands. This is not considered as a bad manner. While you are sitting alone to have your sushi food , you don't need to make use of the chopsticks. You can take sushi foods when you are on a trip just like you are in a restaurant. Some take out restaurants provide fitting dipping cups for the soy sauce.

SUSHI KNIVES

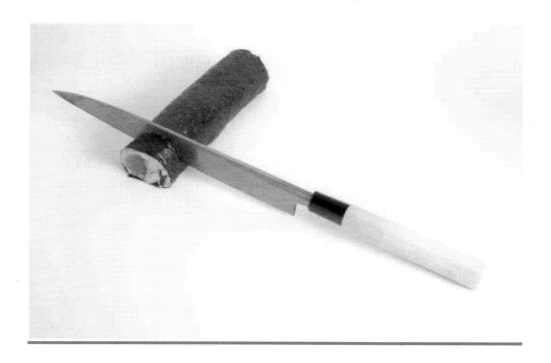

Sushi knives are cutting tools made specifically for making sushi.

They are usually made from the highest quality of carbon steel. This is the same type used in making a "katana," a traditional Japanese sword. The more affordable sushi knives now are made from stainless steel. A sushi knife is differentiated from a regular western knife with its sharpness. Western knives are sharpened on both edges of the blade. A sushi knife, on the other hand, has only one end sharpened. This style is recognized as "kataba."

Because only one end is sharpened, it takes a great deal of precision to perfect cutting sushi or other Japanese food.

Because of this also, there is a different knife for lefthanders.

And lastly, a sushi knife produces cleaner cuts because the food being cut is kept on the sharpened end only. Making sushi is considered an art. Take good care of a sushi knife by following some simple guidelines.

Before using it, always hone a sushi knife. A dull blade will crush a maki. A sharp knife will require little pressure to cut through a sushi.

When cutting "maki," make sure that the blade of your knife is barely wet. It makes sure to produce clean cuts.

It is recommended to first dip the knife tip in water. Turn the knife up so that it points upward, and then tap the handle on the table for water to flow down on the cutting edge. There are many different types of sushi knives depending on a specific cut to be used.

In slicing sashimi, there are three common knives used. First is the yanagi. It looks very much the same as the paring knife of the West. This is mostly used for fish. The second one is the fugu hiki. This is generally used for filleting. The puffer fish is the most common to be filleted. The third sashimi knife is called a yanagi ba. It has long and thin blades that can cut more difficult meat like octopus or squid.

Some fishes can be very large, like a tuna. For this kind, there are special heavy duty knives. It can measure to around 6 feet long and has very sharp blades. Another common sushi knife is the deba bocho. This looks like a carving knife used by Westerns and is wider than a yanagi. Deba bocho is designed for cutting thick meats of big fishes. This can also be useful in cutting through beef and chicken.

Next in the popular line of sushi knives is unagisaki hocho. This is used in filleting fishes like eels. There is a sharp pointed tip specifically designed to take off the heads of eels. The body is shaped like a square and used to slice the meat afterwards.

To cut vegetables, there are two sushi knives usually used. First is the usuba bocho. And the other one is the nakiri bocho. Because of their unique straight edge feature, both knives can slice vegetables very easily without have to push down the blade.

The thin blades make clean and precise cuts without damaging the vegetables. So what is the difference between the two knives? The usuba bocho has only one sharpened edge. Nakiri bocho has both sides sharpened.

7 EASY STEPS TO GREAT SUSHI AT HOME

Making Sushi

When it comes to preparing something tasty, inexpensive, and relatively good for you, I really have to endorse sushi. Sushi is a delightfully delicious bit of Japanese cuisine that can be really intriguing and satisfying to prepare yourself. Going out to sushi bars can be fun, but costs a lot. If you learn how to make your own sushi, you'll be able to save money, eat great and keep the kitchen cool in the summer, because don't forget-sushi uses RAW fish. That means no cooking, which means a nice cool kitchen:)

What You Need

Sushi can have many different ingredients, but usually comprises of a few core ingredients. You'll need special short-grained Japanese sushi rice, nori, (flattened sheets of green seaweed) and ingredients to put in the sushi roll. You'll also need some rice vinegar, sugar and salt to add seasoning to the rice. You can get all of these things at any well-stocked local grocery store except for the nori, which you may need to go to an Asian market for. If you don't live near an Asian market, you can look online for a sushi materials supplier. You will also need a very sharp chef's knife or santoku. A bamboo mat is useful, but not necessary, and can also be found at an Asian grocer. Some common sides for sushi include soy sauce for dipping, wasabi paste (the spicy green stuff!) and pickled ginger (which helps clear the palate between different sushi).

First Step

The first thing you want to do is prepare the sushi rice, since it has the greatest preparation time. You need to rinse the rice very thoroughly and then let it sit in water for around 30 minutes. The soaking allows water to soften the rice grains and will make the rice cook properly.

Second Step

While the rice is soaking is an ideal time to prepare your components. The most common base ingredient is raw fish. Common species used include yellowfin tuna, salmon, squid or eel. Make sure your fish is very fresh (never frozen!) and preferably sashimi-grade. Go to your supermarket and ask if they have sashimi-grade fish. If they doesn't know what you're talking about, go somewhere else. In addition to fish, sushi often contains other ingredients to add different flavors or textures like avocado, cucumber, green onion, cream cheese and spicy sauces. Feel free to get a little crazy when it comes to putting ingredients into your sushi roll, as long as you keep it under 3 ingredients or so. You're going to require around an 8' long strip of each one of your ingredients.

Third Step

Next you need to prepare the rice. The rice should be prepared in a rice cooker which will make perfect rice AND keep your kitchen cool, but if you don't have a rice cooker, you'll have to make do with a microwave or stovetop. Preparing Japanese sushi rice in the microwave can be very difficult and I would strongly suggest you use the stovetop method if you don't have a rice cooker.

Place the rice in a medium sized pot with the water level just slightly above the rice level. Bring the rice to a boil, stirring frequently. Do NOT let the rice stick to the bottom or side of the pan. After the water level is down below the rice level, cover the pot and put it on low heat for 8-9 minutes.

Fourth Step

While the rice is cooking, you can prepare the rice seasoning from the rice vinegar, sugar and salt. It's this mixture that gives sushi rice its notable sweet and sour flavor, so it's very important to get this right, but thankfully, it's not especially to get right. Put all the ingredients in a small saucepan and heat until the sugar and salt dissolve. Do not let the mixture start to boil; it should never get that hot. Stir the mixture to try to make the sugar and salt dissolve fully and then keep it on very low heat until the rice is ready.

Fifth Step

When the rice is done, remove it from the pot into a wooden bowl. Treat the rice carefully-you don't want to crush any of the grains. If any rice is stuck to the side or bottom of the pot, leave it. You don't want any crispy rice in the sushi.

It's important to use a wooden bowl because the vinegar seasoning is about to be poured in and the vinegar may react with the metal. With the rice in the bowl, drizzle the seasoning over it and cut it in (don't stir!) with a wooden spoon. You are just trying to coat the grains of rice with the mixture. If you stir too forecefully, you may damage the grains.

Sixth Step

Let the rice cool for a while. You need cool rice to work with when making sushi. In a sushi restaurant this is generally the time when a chef's assistant will actually fan the rice to help it to cool down more quickly.

Seventh Step

When the rice is cool, take a small hunk of it and spread it over the bottom 5/6ths of the nori, which should be on the bamboo mat if you have one. Nori has two sides, a shiny side and a rough side. Make sure you place the shiny side down. The rice should be spread thinly enough to still see little bits of green through the rice, although you can spread it thicker than that if you have only one ingredient. When you've covered the whole nori sheet except the little bit at the top, you're good.

It helps to spread the sticky rice by keeping a small bowl of water nearby to dip your fingers into, so they don't stick and get messy.

Last Step

Lay your ingredients near the middle-bottom of the nori. Roll up the bottom section of the nori over the ingredients. If you have a bamboo mat, use it to make sure the roll has equal pressure applied on it and is packed tightly. Continue shifting the bamboo mat to roll up more and more of the sushi roll. When you reach the part with no rice, you can roll it over and seal it with a bit of water.

Then, use a sharp knife to cut the sushi roll in half. A slight sawing motion is needed and it helps if the knife is dipped into hot water first.

Double up the two halves and cut THEM in half to make quarters, and each quarter in half to make eighths.

Arrange your sushi rolls on a plate and serve with soy sauce, and wasabi and ginger if you desire.

HOW TO MAKE SUSHI AT HOME:

8 DELICIOUS SUSHI RECIPES

The most basic sushi recipe is not only easy but it is also fun and quick to make. It consists of raw fish like tuna or salmon, sushi rice, seaweed and wasabi. Even though many restaurants pride themselves on making the best sushi or having the best sushi chefs, it should not deter you from making sushi at home. In making your own sushi, you will save money, have fun and add another craft to your list of accomplishments.

1. INARI SUSHI TUNA

Enjoy and savor the delicious delicacy combo of Inari and tuna.

Preparation Time: 24 minutes cooking

Time: 1 hour

Serve: 16 pieces of Inari servings

Ingredients:

- ✓ 1 Pack of Inari
- ✓ 1 Sushi-Grade Tuna or Salmon
- ✓ 3 Big Green Onions
- ✓ 2 Cups of Sushi Rice
- ✓ Sesame seeds(optional)
- ✓ Spicy mayo sauce

Utensils:

- ✓ Bamboo rolling mat
- ✓ Spoons
- ✓ Knife

Preparation:

Open a can of Inari (fried tofu mane into pouches), pick a tofu pouch and slowly open with a carbon steel knife. This must done with utmost care and attention to avoid tearing or piercing the tofu pouch which is fragile.

Carefully fill the hollow portion of the Inari tofu pouches with sushi rice until almost full, but leaving the space for toppings.

Rinse and wash your salmon or tuna. Cut into block and dice into smaller cubes of 1*1 cm.

Wash the three onions. Using a clean knife slice all the onions into rings and transfer into a clean bowl.

Carefully use a spoon to place the diced tuna cubes on the filled Inari pouches

Sprinkle the onion rings on the tuna, sushi rice stuffed Inari pouches. Although optional, you can sprinkle sesame with sesame and mayo sauce to taste.

2.SUSHI NORI ROLLS (seaweeds)

Preparation Time: 30 minutes Cooking

Time: 25 min

Serve: 25 pieces

Ingredients:

- ✓ 5 sheets of nori
- ✓ 2 cups sushi rice(directions indicated below)
- ✓ 2 ounces sushi grade tuna (diced into cubes)
- ✓ 2 ounces of sushi- grade salmon (diced)
- ✓ 1 hot cucumber (Cut into long thin strips)
- ✓ 1 peeled carrot(Cut into long thin strips)
- ✓ 1 avocado (split into two)

Preparation:

Set down a bamboo rolling mat. Carefully place a nori sheet on the bamboo mat with the shiny side up. Place the nori sheet in a way it's an inch away from your own edge of the mat. and make sure there is space on both sides exposing the mate.

Moisten your hand with water to avoid the rice sticking to your palm and scoop a handful sushi rice.

Set the rice down at the center of nori,spread evenly to all side of the nori spread with your fingers. But leave a ¾ inch of rice free space on nori at the far end (opposite side of the mat in front of you).

Wash the avocado and slice into half. Dice one half of the avocado.

Add the sliced avocado, carrots and cucumber already cut into long thin strips but be wary of over filling the nori.

Carefully lift the edge of the rolling mat closest to you and roll away from you to cover the rice and fillings. Simultaneously use your palms and fingers to applied pressure to ensure the content of the mat are firm. Roll over the mat to cover the rice, allowing both sides to join but leaving the ¾ inch side of nori out and exposed. Apply pressure to the rolled bamboo mat to make firm.

Cut the roll in half,further slice each half to make 4 equal pieces. Ready to serve, enjoy!

3.GEFILTE SUSHI

Preparation Time: 24 minutes Cooking

Time: 1 hour

Serve: 10 Wraps of gefilte sushi

Ingredients:

- ✓ Sushi rice
- ✓ A jar of Gefilte fish patty or freshly made gefilte
- ✓ 1 nori sheet

Preparation:

Using a knife carefully cut through the length of the Nori seaweed, long strips (around 2 to 3 cm in width).

Cut the gefilte patty into 3 to 4 slices with respect to the patty size and set in a clean bowl.

Moisten your hand with water and scoop a handful of sushi rice. The moistening will ensure the rice does not stick to your palms.

Mold the rice into firm fingerlike shapes capable of holding thegefilte fish patty.

Place the slice of patty and firm fingerlike sushi rice together. Wrap the patty place on the nori weed with the strip of nori weed. Use a bit of water to close the nori around the rice and patty slice and serve with horseradish.

4. CALIFORNIA STYLED SUSHI ROLL

Preparation Time: 30 minutes

Cooking Time: 1hour

Serve: 8 rolls

Ingredients:

- ✓ ½ pound imitation crab meat
- ✓ 1 ripe avocado
- ✓ Toasted nori seaweed
- ✓ ½ cucumber (peeled and processed into julienne strips)
- ✓ Toasted sesame seeds

Preparation

Toss sesame seeds in a saucepan set over medium heat. Allow to toast while stirring to

 turn golden brown.

Place bamboo sushi mats in plastic trays or wrap. Carefully fold a sheet of nori into half and split. Place the nori on sushi bamboo mat with the rough side of the nori facing up and the smooth side facing down. Moisten your palm and finger to wet before scooping a handful of sushi rice from a bowl and spread them on a half sheet of nori evenly leaving no space.Slightly press the rice into the nori sheet with your finger.

Sprinkle the rice on nori sheet with toasted sesame seeds. Flip the nori sheet upside down and press slightly to make sure the sesame seeds are stuffed to the rice.

The next ingredient to add is the crab meat(kanikarma). But traditionally in theCalifornia sushi roll real crab or crab meat are used. Place two sticks of crab meat in a horizontal position at the center of the flipped nori. Place two slices of cucumber alongside the crab meat in the same position but on the far side of the crab sticks. Next, place three pieces of the avocado on the side closer to you and ensure they are arranged in a well lined row. It's always advisable to put the ingredients on the side nori closer to you. This will ensure all the ingredient stays inside during rolling and will ensure you don't lose sight of the rolling process.

Slide your both of your thumbs under the sushi mat, lift up a bit and use the rest of your fingers to press and hold the fillings in place while you slowly roll the mat towards your fingers. Make sure the edge of the rice closer to you meets the other edge. Apply some pressure to properly mold and compress the roll. Repeat the movement twice. Unroll the mat to reveal the content, a well squared sushi roll. Remove the mate. Using a sharp knife(yanagiba) slightly dampened with water, cut through the roll in 8 pieces starting from the middle. Align each half roll parallel to each other and cut through to make 8 rolls. When cutting sushi it is important to note, don't chop but cut in slow sliding motion.

Serve and enjoy.

5. SALMON NIGIRI

<u>Preparation Time</u>: 20 minutes

<u>Serve</u>: 10 nigiri

<u>Ingredients:</u>

- ✓ Wasabi
- ✓ Pickled ginger
- ✓ 2 cups of cooked sushi rice(seasoned)
- ✓ Fresh salmon, sliced into 10 thin slices
- ✓ Soy sauce to serve.

Preparation:

Sushi is originally a nigiri style which is traditionally sliced fish on top of rice. There are couple of styles to make a nigiri shaped sushi but we will use one of the basic ones here. First dip your hand in vinegar water to make them wet. Having wet hands help the rice to prevent the rice from sticking to your finger while your work with them. The vinegar helps to kill bacteria remaining on your hands or ingredients. Dip your right hand to make it wet,wipe around on your left and slap to splash in order to evenly cover your hands.Prepare sushi rice (as stated in recipe 1) and the best time to use it is about an hour after its cooked.

Thoroughly steamed,but not too wet nor hot. Take a small amount of sushi rice in your palm. Roll and squeeze it together until it rolls into a fine log-sized rectangle. Don't too tight, and make soft enough to contain a little bit of air in the rice. Making a huge difference between rice ball and sushi rice.

Place the fish or a thin slice of salmon on the root of your fingers, using your thumb to lightly hold the top of the fish. So it won't slip off. Add one pinch size of wasabi on the fish and spread evenly.Place the sushi rice you just rolled onto the fish or thin slice of salmon, bend your finger to lightly cover the fish and rice together. Use your index finger and thumb of your right hand to press the rice from top and bottom

Then press down your whole index finger to shape the log. Move your thumb on your left hand to push and turn over the fish or slice of salmon and rice, bringing them onto the first finger joint. Allow the fish or salmon slice to nicely cover the nigiri by shaping the nigiri with your right fingers. Keep those fingers to hold the nigiri and place it on the plate, still using your left hand to lightly press down to make it stable. Shrimps can be used in place of fish. But when using the regular fish make sure to check the right direction of the skin side, because it has a deep cutting edge on the skin side which should always face upwards and repeat the same process earlier mentioned.

Usually nigiri comes in two pieces. When you prepare the second piece put it slightly backwards towards you.

Traditionally there are several reasons for this, first most people are right handed and easier to pick up each pieces of sushi.

This also will make it looks bigger from the customers view point. Serve immediately with soy sauce and pickled ginger to go the side.

6. SPICY TUNA ROLL

<u>Preparation Time</u>: 30 minutes

<u>Serve</u>: 2 rolls

Ingredients:

- ✓ 1 sheet of nori, cut in half crosswise
- ✓ Tezu(vinegared hand dipping water) made from ¼ cup water and 2tspns rice vinegar.
- ✓ Spicy mayo for garnish
- ✓ 2 tbsps of roasted white sesame seeds.
- ✓ ½ tsp sesame oil
- ✓ 2 tspn scallion oil/chopped green onion
- ✓ 3 teaspoon sriracha sauce
- ✓ 2 pounds sashimi-grade tuna
- ✓ 2 cups of prepared sushi rice.
- ✓ Shichimi togarashi (Japanese 7 spice blend)

Utensils:

- ✓ A mixing bowl
- ✓ 1 teaspoon measuring spoon
- ✓ 1 tablespoon measuring spoon.
- ✓ Two spoons for mixing spicy tuna
- ✓ Cutting board
- ✓ A sharp knife
- ✓ Bamboo rolling mat wrapped in cellophane
- ✓ Damp towel
- ✓ A bowl of water

Preparations:

To start we are going to take our block of sashimi grade tuna and slice it up in small pieces. Start by slicing it down the middle, making two layers and vertically slicing into strips that are approximately one centimeter wide. Cut the strip into cubes, divide the tuna cubes into to equal halves of one pound each. Keep aside one pound of tuna cubes for later use, but mince the other one pound of tuna cubes to a much finer texture. You can do that by making movement of your knife in a rocking motion and doesn't have to be neat. Once you are done mincing, transfer it to a mixing bowl. Slice the second half of the tuna into pretty thin (julienne) slices,allow it to have some inconsistent texture for your spicy tuna salad and transfer to a mixing bowl. Wipe of your knife and cutting board. Add spicing ingredients to the tuna in the mixing bowl. Use one table spoon of sriracha for one pound of tuna you are mixing. For two pounds of tuna use two spoons of sriracha. Add your Shichimi togarashi (Japanese 7 spice blend), using half a teaspoon per one pound of tuna but for two pounds of tuna use 1 teaspoon of Shichimi togarashi. Add a half teaspoon of sesame oil to one pound of tuna or make it 1 teaspoon for two pounds of tuna. Mix the content of the mixing bowl using two spoons, one in your left hand and the other in your right hand. Allow the spices to coat the tuna, then toss in the green onions by grab a pinch and sprinkle on the spiced tuna. Mix a little more. The green onions add a nice variety of color. Set the tuna bowl aside and get ready to roll. Unfold the bamboo rolling mat, place the darker side of the bamboo mat face up with the bamboo piece running left to right. Next grab a single sheet of nori or seaweed, fold and cut into half because you will be using half in this recipe. Make sure the rough side of the half seaweed sheet is facing up when you place it on the rolling mat. Get your hand moistened by dipping one hand in the bowl of water and rubbing your hands together. The goal here is to make your hand glossy not dripping with water. Scoop up a handle of rice, spread the rice on top the seaweed. Make sure the rice is four grain thick on the nori and spread to the edges. It's also important to use more of a rolling motion instead of pressing it down because you don't want to smash the rice grains.

Sprinkle some toast sesame seeds on the rice. Get your hands wet again and flip the nori and seaweed by gently lift the nori and rice using the two corners away from you. Add two slices of cucumber in horizontal position and make sure they don't overlap, if they do cut the overlapping part using a knife.

Pick up your bowl of spicy tuna salad and spoon a bit over the cucumber. It's always important to put little less than you think you need in the roll because if you put too much the spicy tuna

They will be push out at the end of the roll or the liquid from the spicy tuna is going to be squeezed out the seaweed during rolling, thus the roll will fall apart one you start to cut it.

Form the spicy tuna around horizontally placed cucumber slices and make it consistent from end to end. Get ready to roll.

Put your two thumbs underneath the bamboo rolling mat, and use your remaining four fingers on each hand to hold on to the spicy tuna. Curl your thumbs up all over the ingredients and continue to roll till you lose sight of the ingredient all together. Squeeze the roll a bit towards you but make sure you don't squeeze too hard so the spice won't come out at both ends. Give it a gentle squeeze and lift the bamboo rolling mat slightly enough so that its no longer in the way. Using one hand pull away from you and with the other hand apply enough pressure downward pressure to keep the bamboo mat up against the rice. Roll your sushi roll over. Check your roll if anything is squishing out of the bottom. If anything is squishing out of the bottom add a little bit of rice to the bottom and cover everything up. Roll that over so that your newly added rice is at the bottom and you can take the bottom part of the bamboo mat and drape it over the top of the roll. Then gently press while simultaneously keeping the top of the bamboo mat rounded. Press slightly and this will conform the newly added rice to the rest of the roll. Now make sure the roll is consistent from end to end and all excess air squeezed out. To ensure the latter move your sushi roll about a inch away from the top of the mat, then drape the bottom of the mat over the top. Using your non dominant hand grab on to bottom part of the bamboo mat and with your dominant hand spread your fingers as wide apart as you can and press down thus allow allowing the top part of the mat touch the bottom part. Make sure not to press down the roll itself. While maintaining affirm grip with one dominant hand and pressing down with the fingertips of your dominant hands, pull the sushi roll back so that it rolls between the two pieces of the bamboo mat. This will tighten the roll a little bit and repair in case of square shape or oblong roll and it will squeeze out all the excess air. Repeat the procedure three or four times. Pick up your sushi roll, set on your cutting board. If you have ingredients squishing out you can drape your bamboo rolling mat over the sushi roll and with one hand on the roll. Get your finger wet and using the edge of the bamboo mat as guide repeat the same process on the other side. Using a knife cut through the middle of the roll using the full length of the knife. Avoid chopping moving movement rather employ consistent back and forth movement with the weight and sharpest part of the knife down to the cutting board. Wipe knife to remove sticking rice or ingredients.

7.<u>SUSHI RICE ROLL</u>

<u>Preparation Time</u>: 50 minutes

Ingredients:

- ✓ 2 cups of white sushi rice
- ✓ Seaweed
- ✓ ¼ lb. raw blue fin tuna, salmon or any saltwater fish
- ✓ Wasabi
- ✓ Soy Sauce
- ✓ Seaweed (optional)
- ✓ Pickled Ginger (optional)
- ✓ Things you need for sushi rice:
- ✓ ½ cup white rice vinegar
- ✓ ¼ cup of sugar
- ✓ 2 teaspoons of salt
- ✓ Konbu Seaweed (as much as desired)
- ✓ 2 large boiling pots
- ✓ Strainer
- ✓ Water
- ✓ Measuring cup

Preparation:

Begin with preparing the sushi rice. Take the two cups of rice and pour it into a strainer. Run water over the rice and rinse thoroughly.

After rinsing the rice, take the rice and place it into one large boiling pot. Fill the pot with the strained rice and water.

The water should completely cover the rice. Soak the rice for at least 20 minutes.

After 20 minutes elapses, drain the water from the pot. Place the rice back into the strainer. Rinse the pot.

Run cold water over the strainer again to rinse the rice

thoroughly until the water runs clear.

Next, place the rice back into

the same boiling pot. Take 2 ¼ cups of cold water and

put the water into the pot with the rice. Heat the water

and rice to a boil. Once boiling begins, reduce heat to

simmer and cover the pot for 20 minutes.

While the rice is cooking, take the ½ cup of white rice

vinegar, ¼ cup of sugar, and two teaspoons of salt and

place into a separate boiling pot.

Let the sugar and salt dissolve in the white rice vinegar

first. Place the seaweed into the pot. Heat the

components on medium heat for at least two minutes or

until seaweed is tender.

After the components are ready, remove from heat and set aside.

After the rice has cooked for 20 minutes, there should be little to no water in the pot with the rice. Remove from heat and let cool for 20 minutes. Once cooled, remove the rice from the boiling pot and place inside a large bowl. Remove the seaweed from the sugar, sale and vinegar mixture and set aside. Take the sugar, salt, and vinegar mixture and pour over the rice.

Thoroughly mix all the components together thoroughly with a large spoon. Now you can begin to assemble the sushi.

Now that the rice is ready, you can begin on cutting the fish. Most traditional sushi recipes call for saltwater fish like salmon or tuna.

Whole, raw blue fin tuna is best suited for this recipe. Take the tuna and slice thin slices. The slices should be no larger than two inches long and ¼ of an inch in thickness. Slice all the tuna you need and put the remaining tuna in a freezer.

Take the wasabi and place a small amount into the center of the tuna slice. You can also add a small strip of seaweed on top of the wasabi.

However, this is optional.

Next, take one small spoonful of sushi rice and fill the tuna with the rice.

Shape the rice and tuna so that the rice does not fall apart.

Don't be afraid to press the rice into the tuna. You can also wrap the tuna slice around the rice if you'd like.

Prepare all the tuna with rice, wasabi and seaweed until you are finished with every piece of tuna. Garnish with soy sauce or pickled ginger to your liking. You may also eat the remaining rice as a side dish.

8.RICE FREE ROLL

<u>Preparation Time</u>: 20 minutes

Ingredients:

- ✓ sheets of nori

- ✓ carrot julienned

- ✓ cucumber julienned

- ✓ A cream cheese guacamole

- ✓ protein of your choice

Preparation:

Put a piece of nori on a piece of waxed paper or sushi Mat.

Spread cream cheese along one end.

This will be the outside end that you close when you roll it.

Spread guacamole in the center of the seaweed.

Place pieces of cucumber and carrot at the opposite end of the seaweed as the cream cheese.

Starting with the veggies, roll the waxed paper to begin rolling the sushi seaweed.

Remove the waxed paper as you go.

When you finish, you should have about a 1.5 inch diameter roll.

Repeat the process with the other sheets of seaweed.

Place all rolls together and cut them into 1 inch pieces.

Keeping them together helps protect the seaweed from breaking when cutting.

Enjoy.

CONCLUSION

Sushi is a tasty food. The combination of rice, seafood and vegetables make the concoction even more enjoyable since the combination of foods satisfies almost every food group. Its decadent taste is only one reason why sushi is good to eat. Another reason to consume sushi is because sushi is also healthy option when consumed in the correct fashion.

Sushi is a healthy option due to the manner in which it is prepared. Since sushi components are uncooked, there are not any fatty additives.

Since there aren't any fats or agents added to sushi during preparation, the sushi also retains more of its healthy components instead of being cooked out.

Moreover, the raw fish in sushi also contains high amounts of Omega 3 fatty acids. These fatty acids are responsible for fighting heart disease and lowering cholesterol. HDL cholesterol, also known as high density lipoproteins, is the healthy cholesterol. When the HDL is raised, the LDL cholesterol or low-density lipoproteins is lowered. LDL is the unhealthy cholesterol which contributes to atherosclerosis and artery blockage.

Omega 3 fatty acids also increase circulation. Circulation may seem insignificant, but circulation is a vital part of diabetes. Although there are few studies that corroborate this evidence, doctors still theorize that the omega 3 fatty acids in sushi benefit those suffering from diabetes patients with poor circulation.

Omega 3 fatty acids also reduce cardiovascular diseases since the acids breakdown cholesterol and improve artery function. The omega 3 fatty acids found in the fish have also be correlated to preventing diseases and treating symptoms in depression, schizophrenia and bi-polar disorder, dementia in Alzheimer's Disease, and joint stiffness and pain associated with arthritis.

Seaweed has all the properties of a super food. Seaweed contains a plethora of minerals, vitamins, riboflavin, iron and calcium. Unlike land grown vegetables, seaweed is extremely potent containing even more beneficial agents than that of traditional vegetables.

Some people do not enjoy the taste of raw food or are concerned when eating raw foods like fish. Studies have shown that consuming raw fish does increase your risk of being exposed to parasites, bacteria and viruses. Also, larger fish have higher mercury levels.

While sushi lovers should take heed of these issues, eating sushi occasionally instead of as a staple meal.

Nonetheless, if you want to reap the health benefits of consuming sushi without being overly concerned with bacteria and parasites, opt for chef prepared sushi instead of store bought or self-prepared sushi. Sushi chefs are professionally trained in handling and preparing sushi at the proper temperature.

Also, don't skip the wasabi when eating your sushi. Wasabi has antimicrobial properties and utilizing it keeps unhealthy bacteria at bay.

In either event, eating sushi is far more beneficial than harmful. Sushi's raw state retains more advantageous components.

Omega 3 fatty acids are among the most helpful agents found in the fish in sushi.

Omega 3 fatty acids increase healthy cholesterol, prevents heart disease, increase circulation in diabetes patients, and even treats life crippling diseases like bi-polar disorder and arthritis.

Kind reader,

Thank you very much, I hope you enjoyed the book.

Can I ask you a big favor?

I would be grateful if you would please take a few minutes to leave me a gold star on Amazon.

Thank you again for your support.

Osami Nishimura

Printed in Great Britain
by Amazon